CHRISTMAS

SATB unaccompanied

OXFORD

See amid the winter's snow

Becky McGlade

MUSIC DEPARTMENT

OXFORD
UNIVERSITY PRESS

See amid the winter's snow

Edward Caswall (1814–78)

BECKY McGLADE

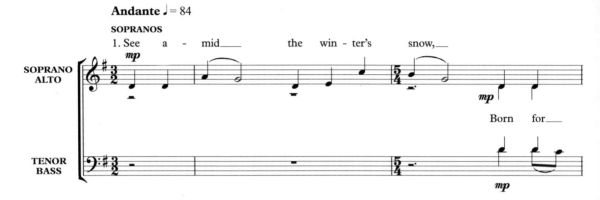

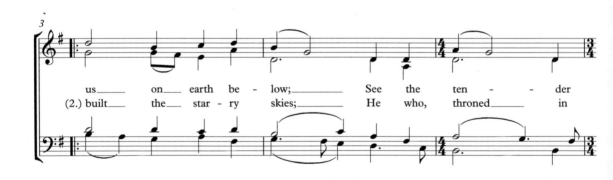

Duration: 4.5 mins

Beth - - le - hem. 3. Say, ye ho - ly shep - herds,

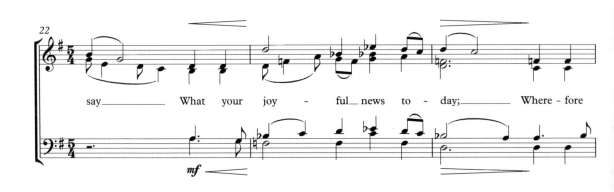

say____ What your joy - ful__ news to - day;____ Where - fore

have__ ye left__ your sheep____ On__ the lone - ly moun - tain

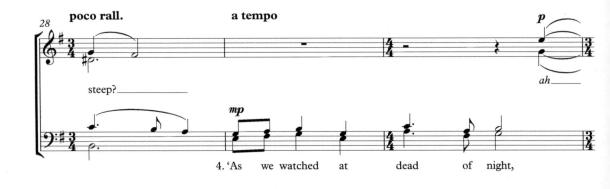

poco rall.   **a tempo**

steep?____

ah____

4. 'As we watched at dead of night,

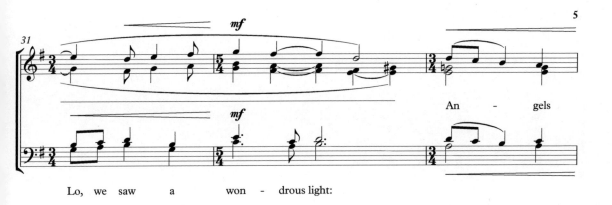

An - gels

Lo, we saw a won - drous light:

poco rall.

sing - - ing___ "Peace___ on earth"___

poco meno mosso　　　　　　　　　　　　**a tempo**

Told us of___ the___ Sa - viour's_ birth.'___ 5. Sa - cred

of the Sa - viour's birth.'___

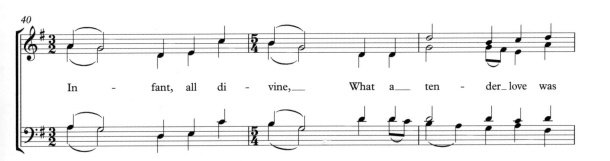

In - fant, all di - vine,___ What a___ ten - der_ love was

thine,_____ Thus to come_____ from high - est_____

bliss_____ Down to such_____ a world___ as

this!_____ Hail,_ thou_ ev - er - bless - ed___ morn!___ Hail, re -

-demp - tion's hap - py__ dawn!__ Sing__ through all__ Je -

-ru - sa - lem,__ Christ is born,____ Christ is__

rall.

in__ Beth - le - hem.

born,____ Christ is born___ in__ Beth - le - hem.

in__ Beth - le - hem.

Music originated by Andrew Jones

OXFORD CAROLS

Oxford publishes a vast array of Christmas music to suit every occasion and choir. There are pieces and collections for services, concerts, and carol-singing; pieces for SATB, upper-voice, and unison choirs; *a cappella* carols and carols with piano or organ accompaniment; and a wealth of traditional favourites alongside new carols by leading composers. There are also over 250 orchestrations of carols from *Carols for Choirs* and other collections available for hire, including versions for brass, strings, and full orchestra. With hundreds of individual titles and an impressive range of carol anthologies, Oxford provides a rich collection of the very best in Christmas music.

Selected carol anthologies from Oxford University Press

Carols for Choirs 1–5

The Oxford Book of Flexible Carols

For Him all Stars, 15 carols for upper voices

A Merry Little Christmas, 12 popular classics for choirs

An American Christmas, 16 carols and carol arrangements from North America

An Edwardian Carol Book, 12 carols for mixed voices

Alan Bullard Carols, 10 carols for mixed voices

Bob Chilcott Carols 1, 9 carols for mixed voices

Bob Chilcott Carols 2, 10 carol arrangements for mixed voices

John Gardner Carols, 11 carols for mixed voices

John Rutter Carols, 10 carols for mixed voices

Mack Wilberg Carols, 8 carol arrangements for mixed voices

Sir David Willcocks: A Celebration in Carols, 18 carols for mixed voices

World Carols for Choirs, SATB and upper-voice editions

Christmas Spirituals for Choirs

The Ivy and the Holly, 14 contemporary carols

OXFORD
UNIVERSITY PRESS

www.oup.com

ISBN 978-0-19-355122-0

9 780193 551220

X816 **See amid the winter's snow** McGLADE